GEOMETRY FOR PRESCHOOLERS

Tracing and Naming Shapes

Children's Geometry Books

Speedy Publishing LLC
40 E. Main St. #1156
Newark, DE 19711
www.speedypublishing.com
Copyright 2017

Let's learn Shapes!

We see shapes everywhere! In our room, school and in our house!

See the chart on the next page to learn these shapes.

CIRCLE
SQUARE
TRIANGLE
PENTAGON
HEXAGON
RECTANGLE
CROSS
TRAPEZIUM
STAR
DIAMOND
QUATREFOIL
ARROW
OVAL
PARALLELOGRAM
OCTAGON
HEART

Have fun with these cool
activities about Shapes!

Enjoy!

TRACE AND COLOR
THAT SHAPE!
Restore the dashed lines.
Color the picture.

Trace and Color!

Trace and Color!

Trace and Color!

Trace and Color!

Trace and Color!

Trace and Color!

EXERCISE 7

Trace and Color!

Trace and Color!

Trace and Color!

EXERCISE 10

Trace and Color!

EXERCISE 11

Trace and Color!

Trace and Color!

Trace and Color!

Trace and Color!

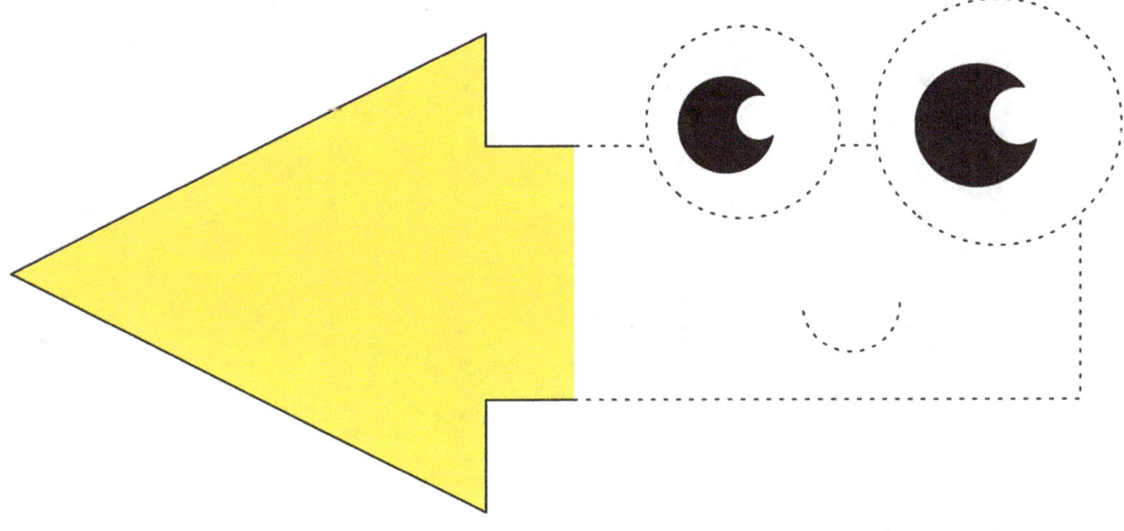

Trace and Color!

FIND THE HIDDEN SHAPE!

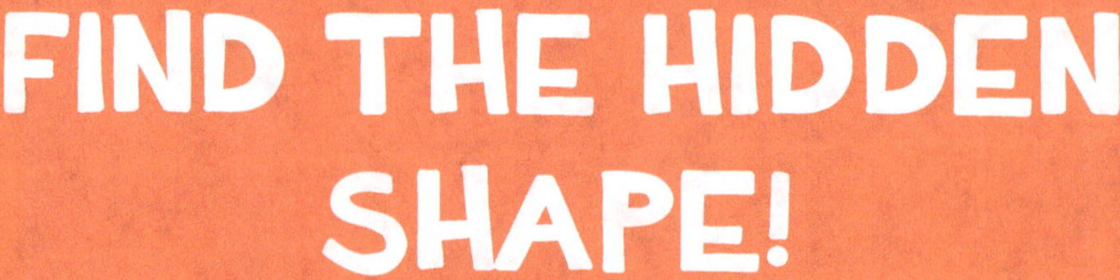

- ➡ Circle the hidden shape.
- ➡ Put a check in the circle beside the correct name of the shape.

Find the Hidden Shape

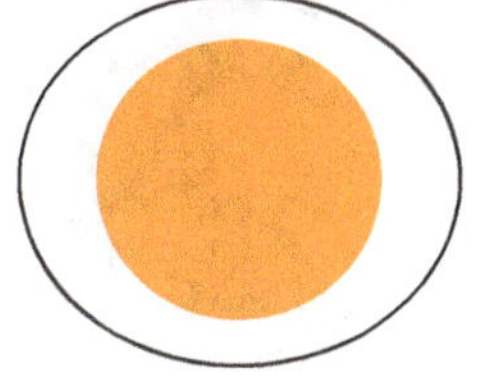

Circle the shape

 CIRCLE

 SQUARE

Find the Hidden Shape

Circle the shape

Find the Hidden Shape

Circle the shape

◯ **CIRCLE**   ◯ **SQUARE**

Find the Hidden Shape

Circle the shape

○ **CROSS**   ○ **DIAMOND**

Find the Hidden Shape

Circle the shape

SEMICIRCLE   TRIANGLE

EXERCISE 6

Find the Hidden Shape

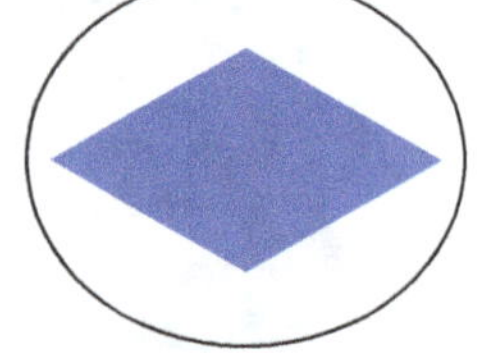

Circle the shape

 DIAMOND

 TRIANGLE

Find the Hidden Shape

Circle the shape

CIRCLE

CRESCENT

Find the Hidden Shape

Circle the shape

CROSS

STAR

Find the Hidden Shape

Circle the shape

⭘ HEART   ⭘ QUATREFOIL

Find the Hidden Shape

Circle the shape

 CROSS

 ARROW

Find the Hidden Shape

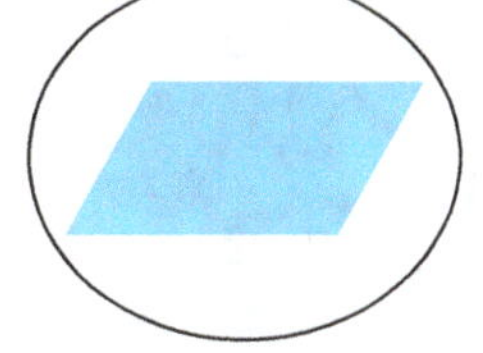

Circle the shape

⭕ RHOMBUS   ⭕ QUAD

Find the Hidden Shape

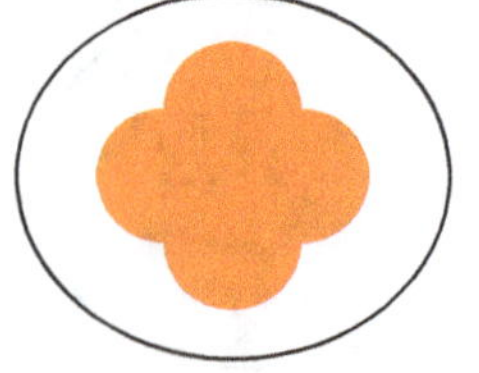

Circle the shape

Find the Hidden Shape

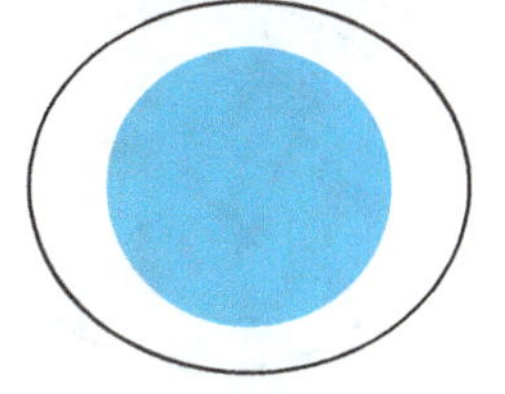

Circle the shape

HEART

CIRCLE

Find the Hidden Shape

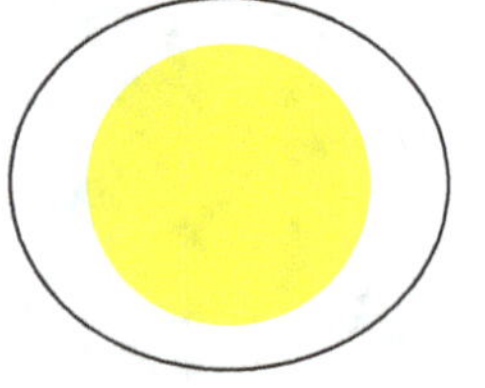

Circle the shape

CIRCLE

ARROW

Find the Hidden Shape

Circle the shape

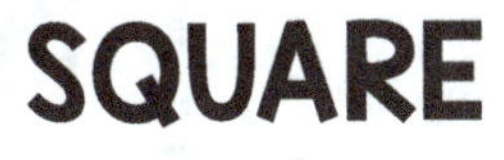

HEART   SQUARE

Find the Hidden Shape

Circle the shape

◯ TRIANGLE   ◯ ARROW

Find the Hidden Shape

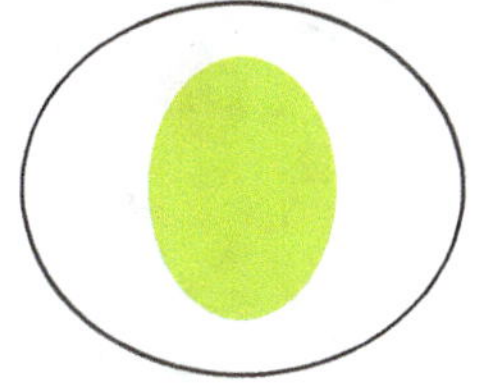

Circle the shape

○ OVAL   ○ CIRCLE

EXERCISE 18

Find the Hidden Shape

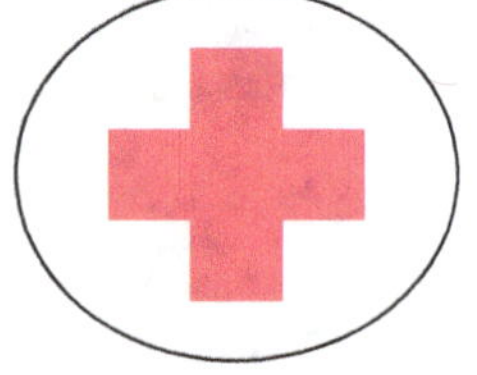

Circle the shape

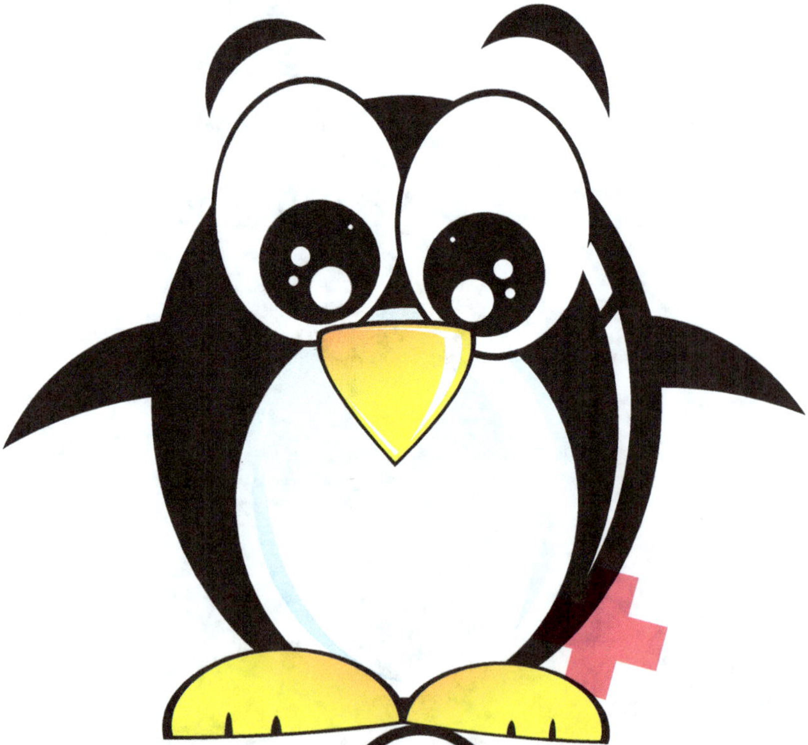

◯ SEMICIRCLE ◯ CROSS

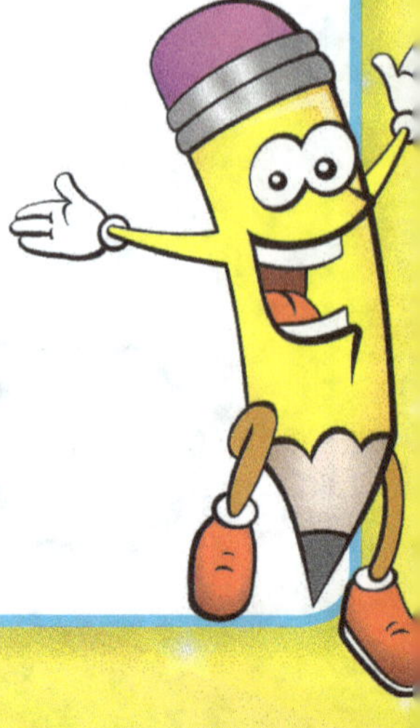

CUT AND PASTE

➲ Cut out the shapes at the bottom of each page.

➲ Paste them beside the matching shapes.

EXERCISE 1

Cut out the graphics at the bottom of the page and glue them to the matching shapes.

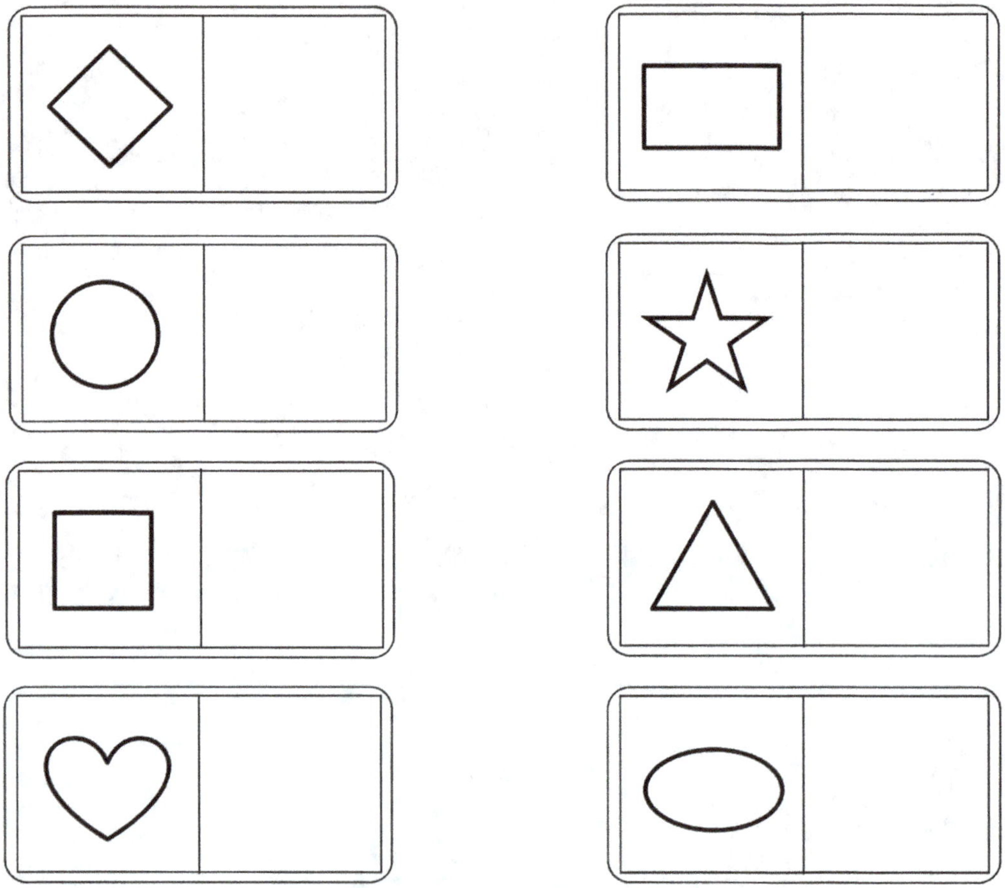

Cut out the graphics at the bottom of the page and glue them to the matching shapes.

for cutting purposes only

EXERCISE 3

Cut out the graphics at the bottom of the page and glue them to the matching shapes.

EXERCISE 4

Cut out the graphics at the bottom of the page and glue them to the matching shapes.

for cutting purposes only

EXERCISE 5

Cut out the graphics at the bottom of the page and glue them to the matching shapes.

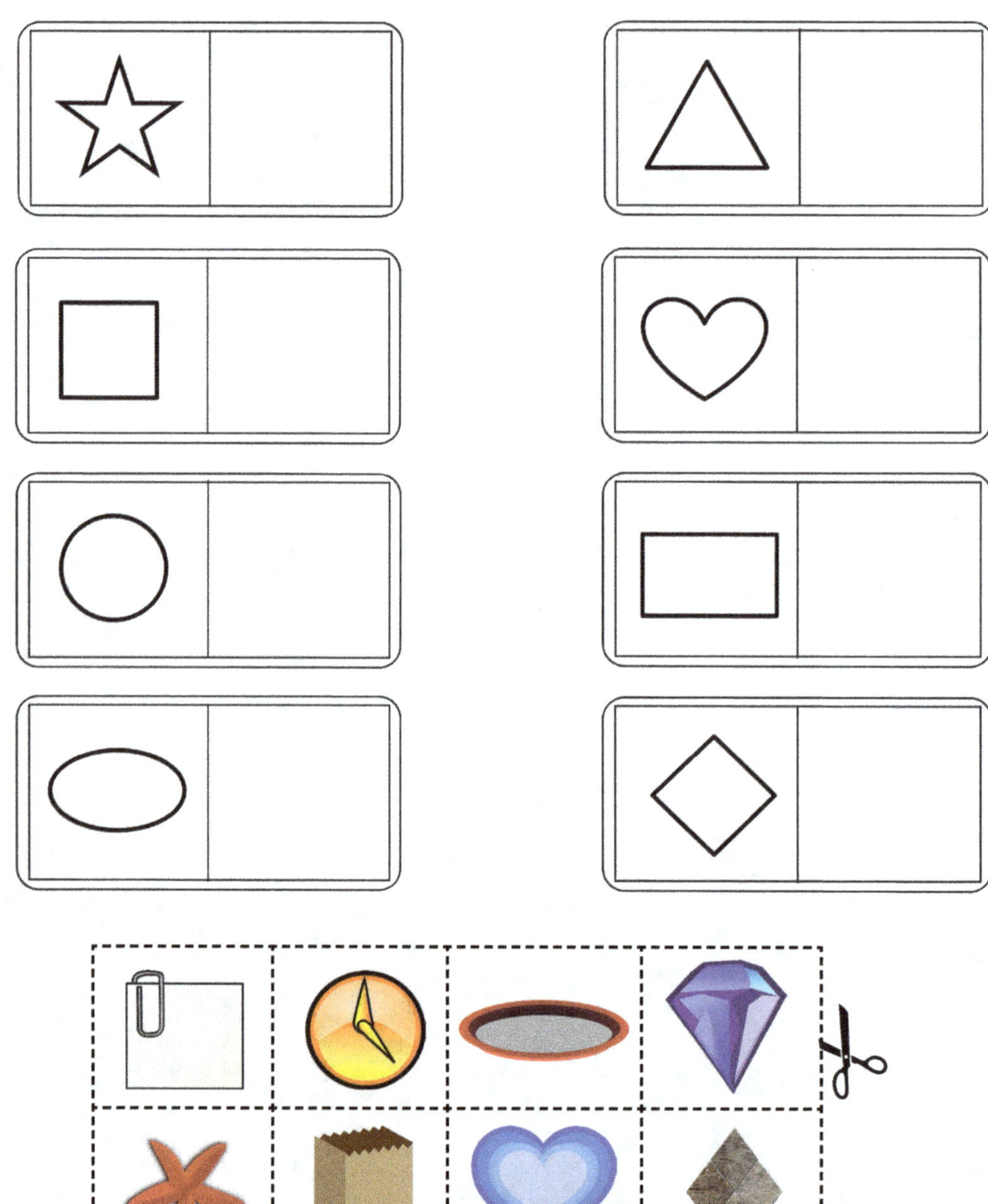

GOOD
JOB!

ANSWERS

EXERCISE 1
Find the Hidden Shape
Encircle the shape
CIRCLE

EXERCISE 2
Find the Hidden Shape
Encircle the shape
SQUARE

EXERCISE 3
Find the Hidden Shape
Encircle the shape
SQUARE

EXERCISE 4
Find the Hidden Shape
Encircle the shape
CROSS

EXERCISE 5
Find the Hidden Shape
Encircle the shape
TRIANGLE

EXERCISE 6
Find the Hidden Shape
Encircle the shape
DIAMOND

EXERCISE 7
Find the Hidden Shape
Encircle the shape
CRESCENT

EXERCISE 8
Find the Hidden Shape
Encircle the shape
STAR

EXERCISE 9
Find the Hidden Shape
Encircle the shape
HEART

EXERCISE 10
Find the Hidden Shape
Encircle the shape
ARROW

EXERCISE 11
Find the Hidden Shape
Encircle the shape
parallelogram

EXERCISE 12
Find the Hidden Shape
Encircle the shape
QUATREFOIL

EXERCISE 13
Find the Hidden Shape
Encircle the shape
CIRCLE

EXERCISE 14
Find the Hidden Shape
Encircle the shape
CIRCLE

EXERCISE 15
Find the Hidden Shape
Encircle the shape
SQUARE

EXERCISE 16
Find the Hidden Shape
Encircle the shape
TRIANGLE

EXERCISE 17
Find the Hidden Shape
Encircle the shape
OVAL

EXERCISE 18
Find the Hidden Shape
Encircle the shape
CROSS

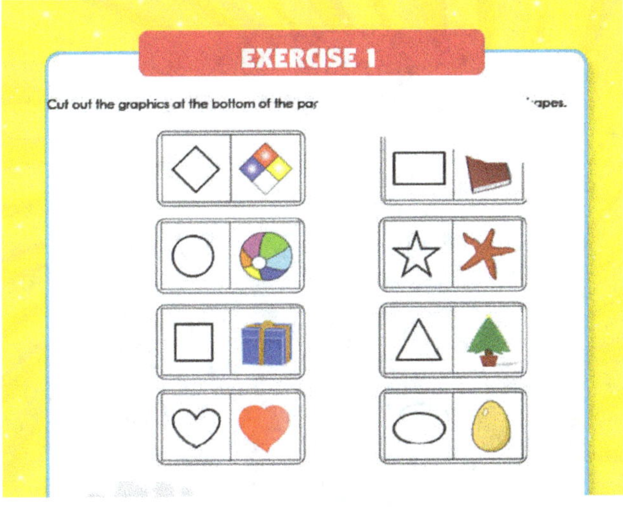

EXERCISE 1
Cut out the graphics at the bottom of the par

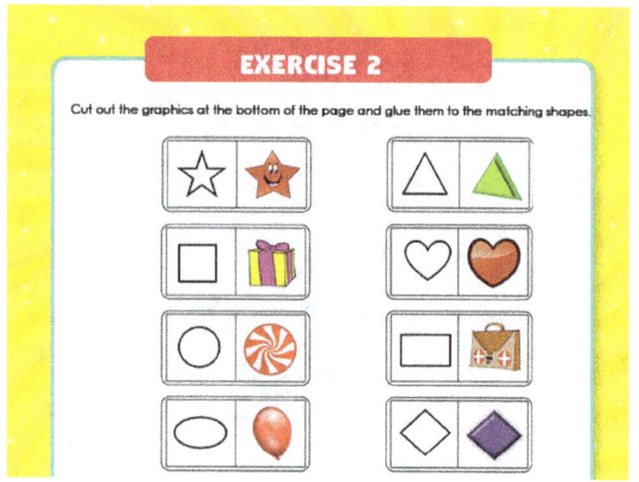
EXERCISE 2
Cut out the graphics at the bottom of the page and glue them to the matching shapes.

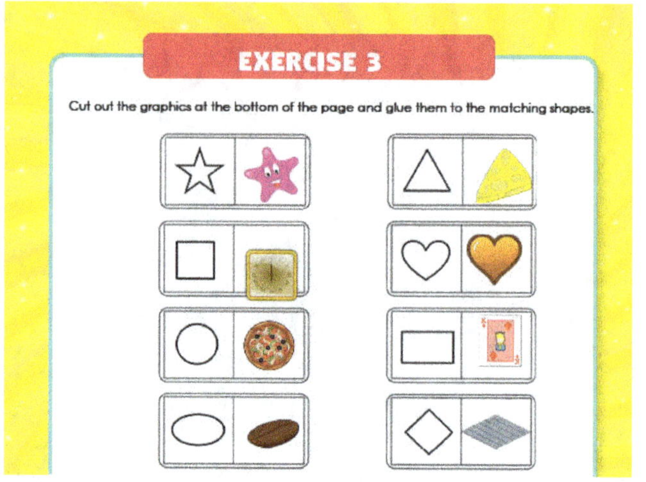
EXERCISE 3
Cut out the graphics at the bottom of the page and glue them to the matching shapes.

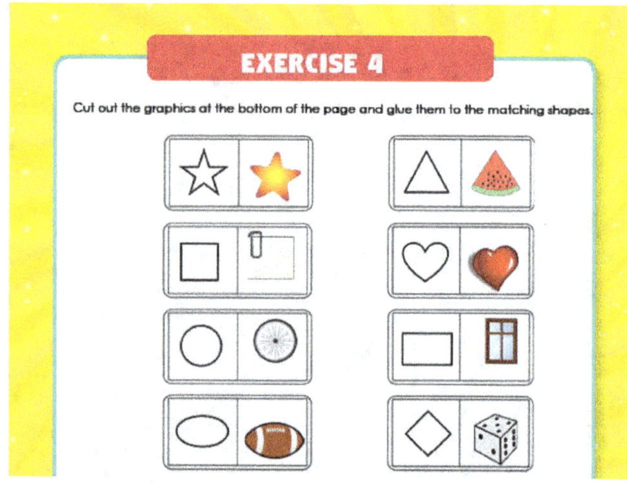
EXERCISE 4
Cut out the graphics at the bottom of the page and glue them to the matching shapes.

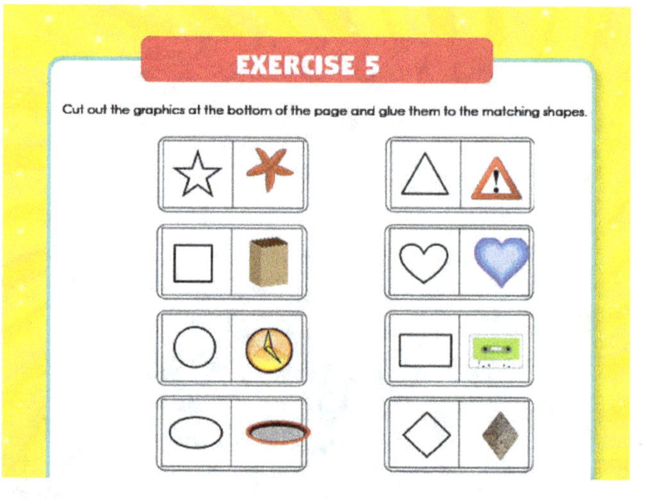
EXERCISE 5
Cut out the graphics at the bottom of the page and glue them to the matching shapes.

Visit

BABY PROFESSOR
EDUCATION KIDS

www.BabyProfessorBooks.com
to download Free Baby Professor eBooks
and view our catalog of new and exciting
Children's Books